With a Gift for Burning

poems by

Laura Apol

Finishing Line Press
Georgetown, Kentucky

With a Gift for Burning

Copyright © 2018 by Laura Apol
ISBN 978-1-63534-402-8 First Edition
All rights reserved under International and Pan-American Copyright Conventions. No part of this book may be reproduced in any manner whatsoever without written permission from the publisher, except in the case of brief quotations embodied in critical articles and reviews.

ACKNOWLEDGMENTS

Several of these poems first appeared in various forms in the following:

ERRANT; THE FIRE; and AFTERBIRTH in *Imagine This: An Artprize Anthology* 2013
EASTER SUNDAY, MY MOTHER in *Imagine This: An Artprize Anthology* 2014
MIDWINTER, MY MOTHER in *The Briar Cliff Review*
DAUGHTER LEAVING HOME in *Teasing the Tongue: A Wintergreen Anthology*

Publisher: Leah Maines
Editor: Christen Kincaid
Cover Art: Rod Hoekstra
Author Photo: Michael McPeak
Cover Design: Elizabeth Maines McCleavy

Printed in the USA on acid-free paper.
Order online: www.finishinglinepress.com
　　　　　　also available on amazon.com

Author inquiries and mail orders:
Finishing Line Press
P. O. Box 1626
Georgetown, Kentucky 40324
U. S. A.

Table of Contents

BIRTHRIGHT 1

MOTHER, SMOKING 2

MIDWINTER, MY MOTHER 4

VEINS 5

ERRANT 6

AFTERBIRTH 7

EASTER SUNDAY, MY MOTHER 9

ON MY FIFTIETH BIRTHDAY, I RETURN 10

A PHOTO 11

DAUGHTER LEAVING HOME 12

THE FIRE 13

NOVEMBER RAINS 14

ATTACHMENT 15

LOSS 16

RESURRECTION 17

FEBRUARY 29TH 18

THE GIFT OF *YES* 19

*For my mother, Gladys
and my daughter, Hanna*

If I'm lonely
it's with the rowboat ice-fast on the shore
in the last red light of the year
that knows what it is, that knows it's neither
ice nor mud nor winter light
but wood, with a gift for burning
—Adrienne Rich, "Song"

BIRTHRIGHT

Saturdays, my mother
took me to her mother:

rose patterns on china, dish towels
cross-stitched with days of the week;
a rat-tailed comb, brush curlers,
pink hair-set tape,
and Dippity-Do.

I dusted mopboards,
shook rugs and polished silver
while my mother, stiff with silence,
washed and styled her mother's hair.

The house smelled of setting gel,
rose water and rage—
ghost tongues weary of their stories.

Decades later, my daughter
learned to polish
my mother's nails; I buttoned
her blouse, teased her hair.
Each visit bore the tarnish
of never-enough.

Now I live alone by a river.
My daughter seldom calls;
I rarely answer.
Only the salmon return
each autumn, doubling back
to the stream they were born in.

Along the banks, cattails explode
—a thousand furred tongues.

MOTHER, SMOKING

How could I know that a woman
whose hands could no longer button her blouse
could hold a smoke—hold a smoke till it drops
past the wheels of her chair to the bathroom rug?

How could I know that a woman
whose hands could no longer sign her name
could take a drag—take a drag till it drops
past shoes she is unable to tie?

~

That house was filled with smoke—
the holy ghost with yellowed fingers,
blackened lungs, water and wine.

A smoker himself,
my father would not be married
to a woman who would light up. So she swore
she had quit, and he went on buying denial
twenty menthols at a time.

When she was no longer able,
he helped her to the bathroom,
held the Salem to her lips, betrayal
in every draw.

Put out your hand, father. The lit tip
stubbed into your palm is hot as a nail.

~

Ash, then, was my inheritance—fallen
from her secret cigarettes, her black-tar affair
of more than fifty years.

This is the blaze that blackens the photos,
me the choked child who tried not to notice
the lipstick-ringed filter in the toilet, prayed
not to smell smoke.

Watch the house burn, child. Watch the split-level
house in flames.

Ashes, ashes. We all fall down.

MIDWINTER, MY MOTHER

After I left the cemetery, I drove—
east to the ocean, seven states away.
The journey was slow, weighted as I was,
myself in my arms. I thought
she would go with me. I thought
she would stay with me in my sleep. Instead,
I dreamed of fallen horses, ruins of battle
—those useless limbs, those dying horses'
eyes. I walked on the beach
until I understood: how water and time
grind down the world, hand us our cartilage,
broken. Hand us our bones.
She'd understood, in the end,
because I had to tell her. I stood by her bed,
kept my mind on the moon, the clear
winter light. I wanted to hear her say
she loved me then, and I pretended she did,
pretended to hear those words in the waves—
above shards of shell, fish bones
picked clean.

VEINS

The veins on my legs
are my motherline, a blue umbilicus
stretching from my grandmother
through my mother
to the thick purple blossoms
on the curves of my calves, indigo
tendrils, violet bouquets,
and the only day the doctors
can laser them invisible
is the third Wednesday of October
—my mother's birth day, grief
the hot needle searing to scars
the flowers I would place on a table,
a hospital bedside, a grave.

ERRANT

The teen-aged daughter
who last night reminded me
I know nothing about anything,
      and most of all nothing about her,

this morning decided
I might know something after all.
I might know where her earring landed
when it fell as she ran distance
yesterday after school.

No ordinary charm—
a gift just that morning from the first boy
to give her a token of any sort.
I imagine him, half her height,
holding out the small blue box;
imagine her smile, her pleasure, all that light.

So I find myself
in the field behind her school
searching the chill for one errant earring,
as if she might be right and a mother can intuit
where a sterling hoop lies hidden in the grass.
It is the first morning of frost,
and every blade is stiff,
      silver-white and shining.

I pace the edge of the field
with measured steps,
      —forward, back—
scanning for silver against the rising sun,
thinking of my daughter as she runs—
her lean strong legs,
      her tangled white-blond hair.

AFTERBIRTH

I rise in the dark to a full morning
moon. My daughter's eighteenth birthday,
and I am bleeding as I did
in the days after she was born.
Now, as then, my empty womb contracts.

Outside her room, I pause
to hear her breathe, even and steady,
think of the ways she has shared
my blood: all I tried to give her,
all I could not keep her from

—the way I told time
before her birth (in five moons, the baby
will be born; in two moons, the baby
will be born);

—my shuffling walks
down hospital hallways, my newborn
in my arms, as I murmured
I have a daughter, I have a daughter.

Her father and I vied for her
from the start, each of us wanting
the woman she would become. She started
her cycles linked to mine—two women
tuned to the same lunar score, her young
body following, then eclipsing my own.

When, on his yearly visits, her father
tried to blunt her blossoming, she turned
her rage on me: wanting, not wanting
to be home; wanting, not wanting
to be held.

So I sit on the porch in the early
hush, sifting our splintered past. Nearby,
a nightbird cries, and I step
to the door. There, in the bare arms
of the elm, a dark bundle rests:
a Great Horned Owl—

such insistent calls, such loud silence
in between. From her perch, she spreads
her wide-shadow wings, catches
the breaking light and—rising—
blots out the blood-red dawn.

EASTER SUNDAY, MY MOTHER

I knew she would come to me in the spring,
not as a heron or owl or steady cardinal flame,

but as a flash, years in the making—a moment
my hunger could not afford to miss.

And so I put out feeders, bulging with seed.
It was the year everything bloomed

too soon or not at all, the year
of extravagant finches: I couldn't get over

how yellow they flew. When the calico
brought gilded feathers to the door,

I knew what I loved was truly gone.
Still, those feathers littering the steps

were not without grace, which meant
I could love the finch—frail, electric petals

of light. But I could love, too, the cat,
taking and giving in equal measure,

and love as well those aching feathers,
warm in my palm.

ON MY FIFTIETH BIRTHDAY, I RETURN

The street, the market,
the church on the corner—how can I turn back
the trees? There would have been
leaves, this yellow, and light, and the same
October air. A woman rose that day, felt
the stretch of her skin and a baby's kick,
breasts tender, back swayed. These motes in the air:
is this all that remains? The body that held me
is gone; brick-solid, the garage apartment
where she slept and woke. These sills
hold that morning: her breath at the window,
her bent-double prayers. The stoop
where she stood, the stained concrete steps—
how can I turn back the sky?

A PHOTO

My daughter is off to her last day of school,
ever. In her miniskirt and heels, eyes rimmed
black, lips red,

she is all about her missing calculus book, pack
hoisted to her shoulder as she marches out,

rejecting even this moment of ritual:

each fall, first day of school—photo on the porch:
each spring, last day of school—photo on the porch.

Thirteen years should mean thirteen pairs of photos,
now less one.

I picture the shots in a line, season in, season out,
everything a blur between—my failures, glyphs
in her growing bones, in the cells of her changing
hair and baby-to-permanent teeth,

the prints growing clearer each year.

Her dreams faltered long ago, her world harsher
than I imagined, and we have—each of us—paid.

So this morning offers no porch smile,
no bitter-sweet tears. No click of a shutter—
just a door slammed shut.

DAUGHTER LEAVING HOME

I love the word *fragile*, love
    the word *tensile*—

and how, in stretching, some things
are both.   Some things

    are not.

Once on windy Bowen
I saw a spider's web—

      spun silk
    buoyed between branchings,

      shining wet
    with end-of-summer dew—

and tried to fix it
in a photo.   With just the breath
of my approach

it ruined.

    What am I saying, then?

The late fields are yellowing. Here
and there,   a leaf turns.

Each hummingbird
    may be the season's last

—so much distance
    in a sky this blue.

THE FIRE
> *When you do something, you should burn yourself*
> *completely, like a good bonfire, leaving no trace.*
> *—Shunryu Suzuki*

I draw solace from this solitude,

the labyrinth of desert grass and dried
creek beds, the absolution
of the morning stars. Here, the world
forgives—

until my distant daughter
rises from the hard red dirt, wings
white with ash. She reels me
in on the taut umbilical of care:

why didn't you why can't you why won't you
love me? And then my own, *how could I*
not?

Once, I mapped the moons
toward when she would be born—

held her in my ache until she broke
my stretched embrace, emerged
hand-first. Even then she could not wait
to leave.

Now her rage consumes us;
flinted words throw sparks, savage fingers
flare. She points her fierceness
across miles and years and

—tinder that I have become—for her,
I burn.

NOVEMBER RAINS

If my daughter were here, I would
walk with her into this grey and heartless
day, show her where a half-moon
curve of woven grass is cradled
in the crook of the oak, or sheltered
beneath the eaves. A nest can withstand
wind, and winter, I would say. It waits,
upturned—a begging hand.

ATTACHMENT
—at the Buddhist Temple Borobudur

I walk in silence, circling
each level of the temple sunwise
three times.

It is a lesson in cut stone,
in carvings, in bell-shaped *stupas*
that point the way

to heaven, each step
a practice in loosening attachment
and desire.

The guide says
on the seventh level I can make
my personal request for blessing.

I circle and climb. Circle
and climb. With each footfall,
I hold my daughter

in my mind. Yesterday
at the *Pièta*, I lit a candle.
Tomorrow, I will cover my head,

bare my feet in the mosque.
I am searching for an ear
that listens.

Like the saffron-robed monks,
bowing with each step, I hold
and let go.

LOSS

It is hard to hold
what you have:
        too much weight
        on one side of the scale.

It is in loss
that something is noticed:
        the eye drawn to the empty
space,   the ear hearing only
an absence
        that clamors.

Think of the bare spot
        on the wrist,
the sweater left
        draped on the back
                of a chair.
Think of the daughter
who does not write.

The widow's coin, the lamb that slipped
the fold—

if what is lost
later is found,
        it is a treasure,
        seen new.

RESURRECTION

A she-bear comforts me in the morning dream
two years after my mother's death, climbs
onto the shabby sofa of my childhood,
covers me with heavy limbs, warm breath. I lie
still under her. It is winter, wind
howling down the chimney, the fire
cold. The river has broken

into large floes that drift downstream,
ice buckling onto itself, all fissures and folds.

~

My mother never wanted to be buried
in frozen ground, but at the cemetery
we had to make our way across drifts, gullies

of snow, hunched against the wind. Is it true
believers are buried with their feet to the east,

so when they are raised they face Christ, the risen
sun? I picture her now, a Sunday school painting—
suddenly upright, face alight, frozen earth
ruptured and falling away.

~

All week, I have looked for an eagle circling.
The skies are silent. There are deer,
and the tracks of deer. A lone fox.
And an ice bird on the snow—russet wings,
a wild tuft and ruddy beak.

Open the window. Let the red bird in.

FEBRUARY 29TH

The snow arrives at dawn,
        white on white:
smoke from the woodstove,
              ice on the river.

All day I watch
for you. Four years, the leap of time
             from your death
        to this day. Then, too, snow

obscured the picture—
        mother-in-my-mind
with whom it would take decades
to make peace.

But I want a sign.
      I want a sign
that things are right with us now.

I want to believe
            in an afterlife

where you hold out your arms to me,
        wide as the wings
        of the swan I am not able to see
until,
        from the white river, it rises

                into the storm
                      of this blinding day.

THE GIFT OF *YES*

I tell my mother I want to
go to the lake, waterskiing with friends,
instead of to Sunday service

and this time she does not say,
>*Laura, you know how we feel about this.*

She does not say,
>*You can make up your own mind.*
>*But you know how we feel about this.*

She does not say,
>*My mother would never have let me go,*
>*but you can make up your own mind.*
>*And you know how we feel about this.*

Instead, she says,
Yes. Have a good time. And here's some money
for ice cream—

and in that moment

her own mother hands me suntan lotion and a hat,
her sister tosses me a towel,

and with her gift of *yes*, my mother
climbs in beside me in the back.

Laura Apol teaches creative writing and literature in the College of Education at Michigan State University. For more than twenty years, she has led creative writing workshops in local, national and international contexts for writers of all skill levels.

Her poetry has appeared in a number of literary journals and anthologies, and she is the author of several collections of her own poems: *Falling into Grace; Crossing the Ladder of Sun* (winner, Oklahoma Book Award for Poetry); *Requiem, Rwanda* (finalist, Lascaux Prize in Poetry; drawn from her work using writing to facilitate healing among survivors of the 1994 genocide against the Tutsi, and translated into Kinyarwanda under the title *Emwe N'imvura Irabyibuka* [*Even the Rain Remembers*]); and *Celestial Bodies* (winner, Overleaf Chapbook Manuscript Competition and finalist, Oklahoma Book Award).

Her full-length poetry collection, *Nothing but the Blood*, is forthcoming from the Michigan State University Press, and she is currently completing a novel-in-poems, *Tutsi*, based on her work in Rwanda.

More information is available at her website: laura-apol.com

www.ingramcontent.com/pod-product-compliance
Lightning Source LLC
LaVergne TN
LVHW041523070426
835507LV00012B/1776